The Usborne Little Children's

KNIGHTS & CASTLES Activity Book

Rebecca Gilpin

Designed and illustrated by

Erica Harrison

Laurent Kling, Fred Blunt,
Mattia Cerato, Cecilia Johansson,
Vincent Bergier, Benedetta Giaufret,
Enrica Rusinà and Erica Sirotich

Edited by Fiona Watt

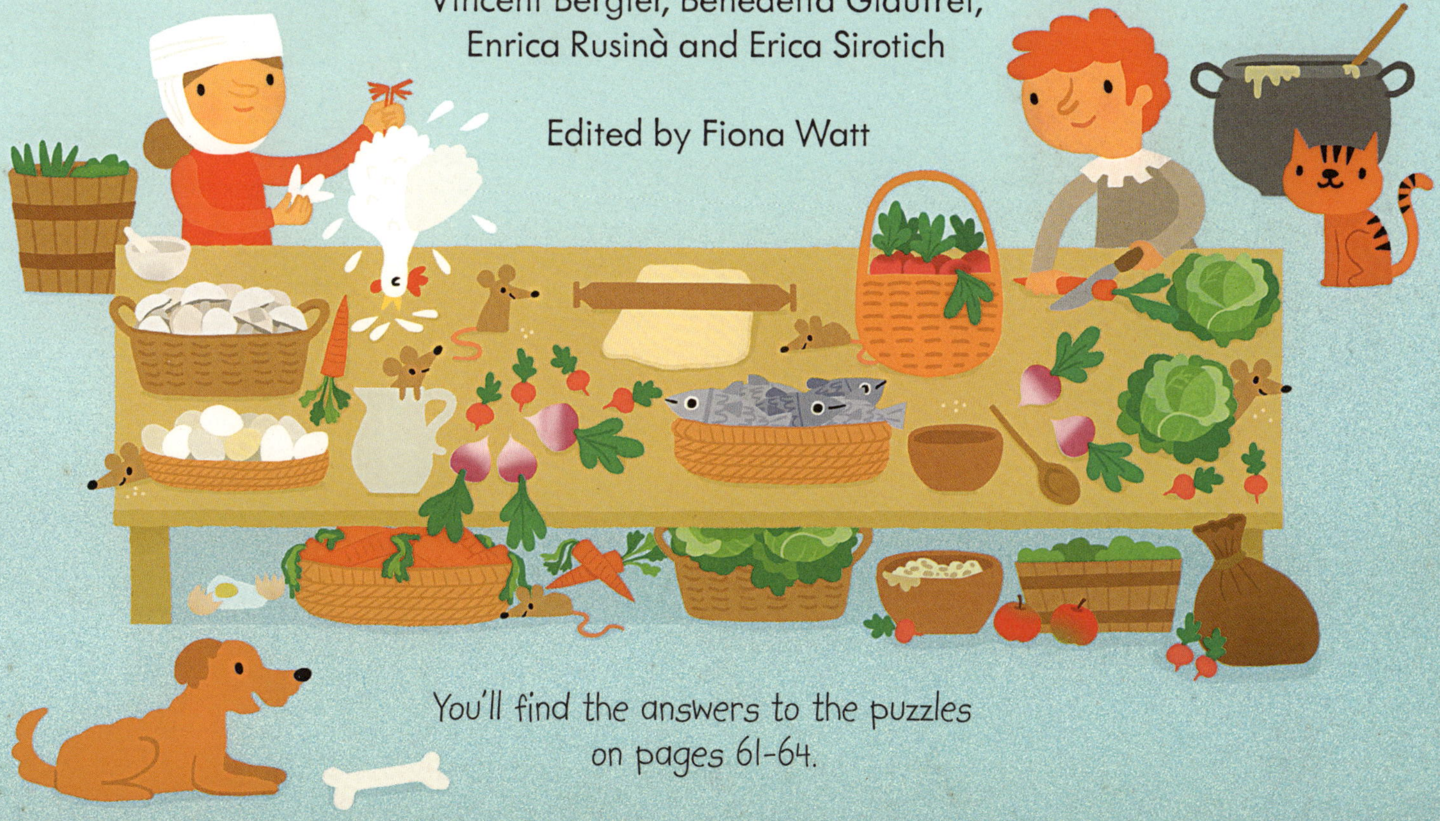

You'll find the answers to the puzzles on pages 61-64.

A strong fortress

Which tower is tallest?
Write A, B, C or D here: ....

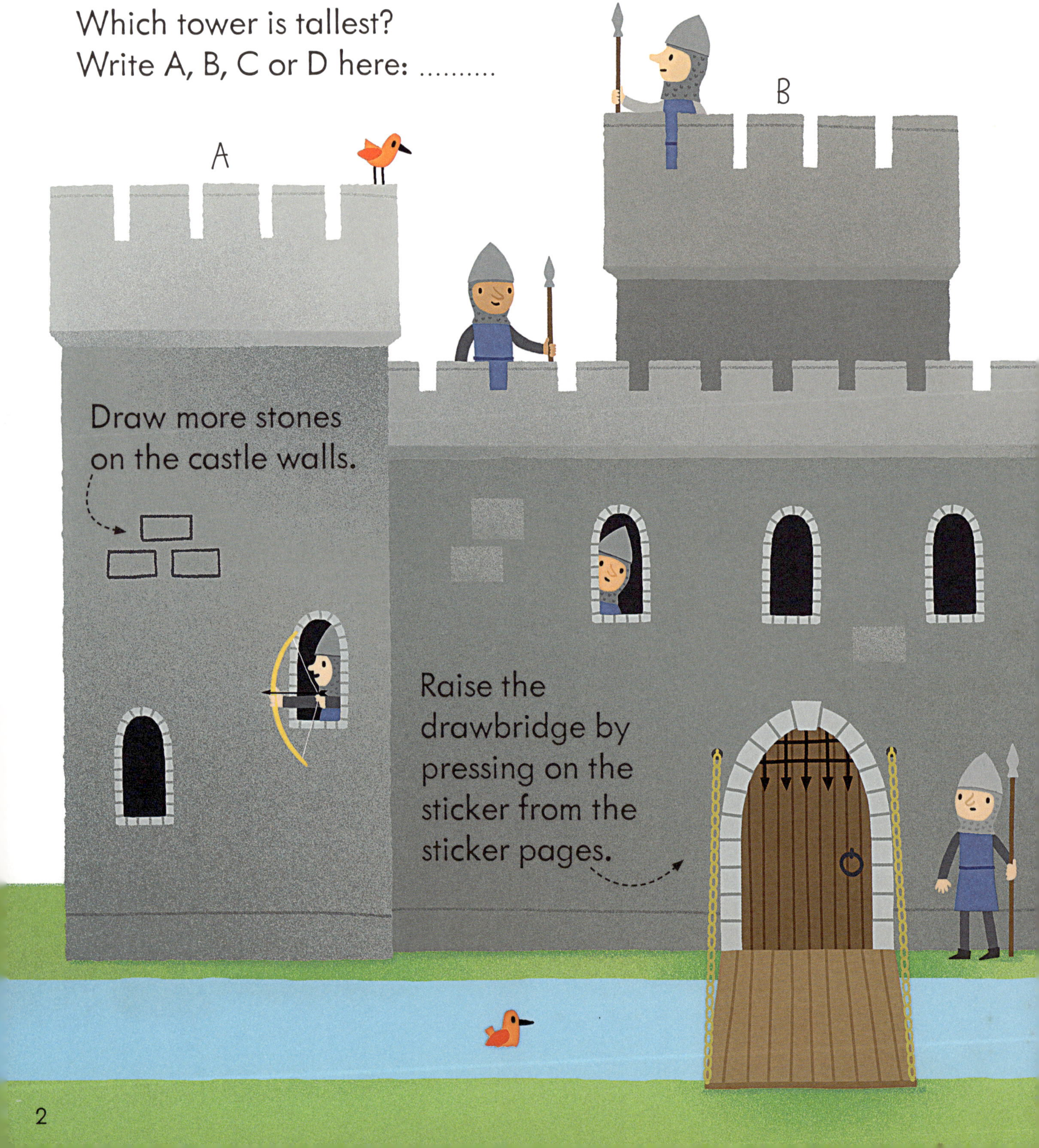

Draw more stones on the castle walls.

Raise the drawbridge by pressing on the sticker from the sticker pages.

Can you spot a lady looking out of a window?

Add more birds in the sky.

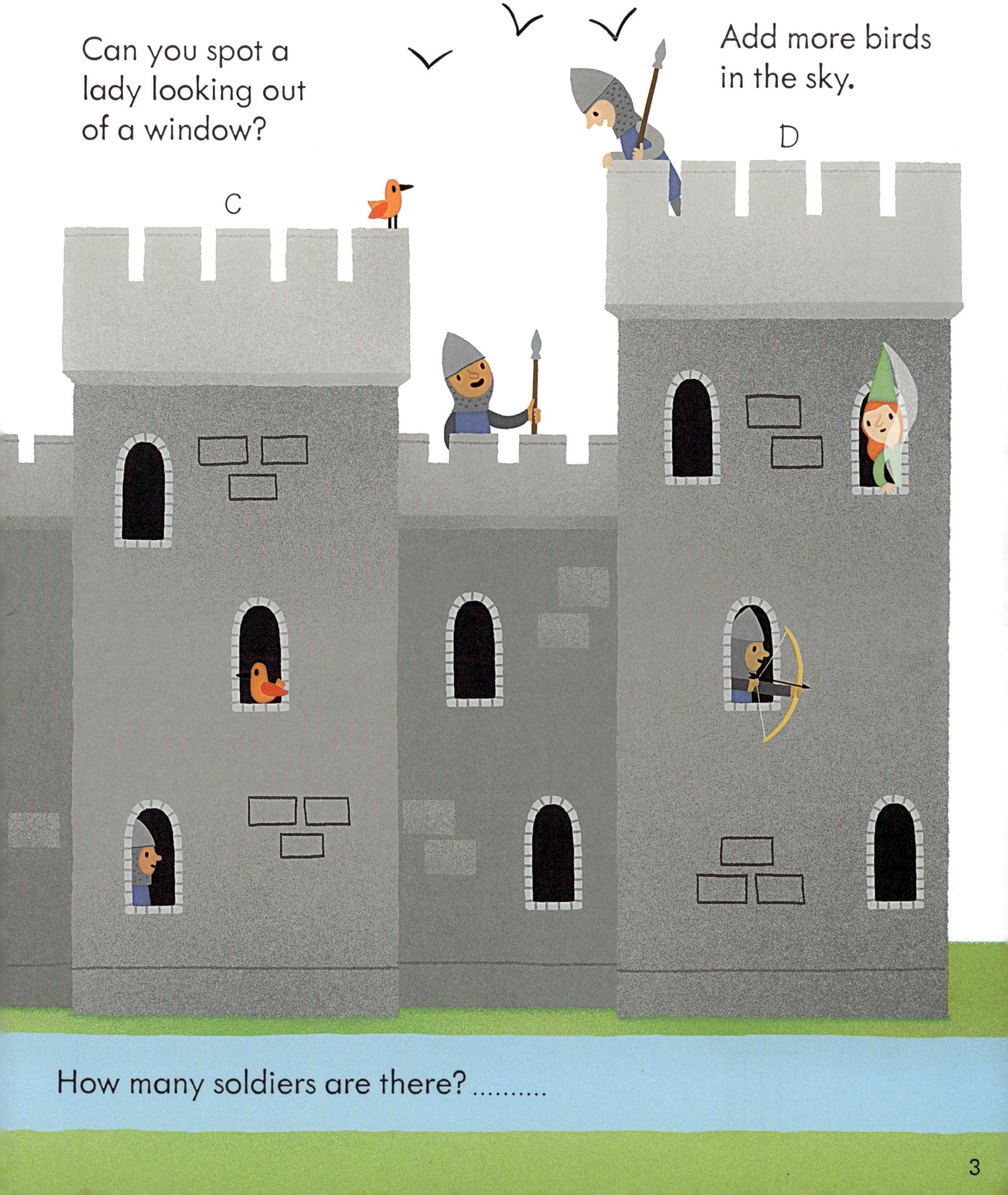

How many soldiers are there? ....

Draw a knight...

1. Draw a body. Add a teardrop shape above it.

2. Draw a helmet, then add a face.

3. Draw a shield and an arm with a sword.

4. Draw two legs. Colour the knight.

Draw more knights and ladies in this space.

...and a lady

1. Draw a shape for a dress. Add a circle for a head.

2. Draw hair and a face. Add a line for a belt.

3. Draw two arms and hands. Add two feet.

4. Draw a hat, then add a veil. Colour the lady.

Out and about

Which knight is going to the castle?

Draw the door and add windows, stones and flags.

Complete the rest of the trees in the forest.

To draw a castle, follow the white line without taking your pen off the paper.

Start here.

Draw a line along the path as quickly as you can, to take this knight to the village. Try not to bump into the sides.

Busy courtyard

Can you spot these people?

a man chopping wood

a woman with a *basket*

children playing with a *ball*

a *busy* blacksmith

How many of each of these can you see?

bucket ....

dog ....

well ....

goose ....

Do you think it would have been quiet or noisy in this castle?

....

Lots of castles

There were many different kinds of castles. Find the castle stickers on the sticker pages, then stick each one on the shape it matches.

A rich knight wants to visit all three of his castles.
Draw a line that will take him to a castle with two towers, then to a castle with a moat, then to a castle on a hill.

How many trees does he pass? ....

Does he cross a stream? YES / NO

Castle supplies

A farmer is bringing supplies to a castle. Read the list below and look at the picture. Is anything missing? YES / NO

- a sack of flour
- a pig
- a bundle of hay
- a basket of carrots
- wooden logs
- a bag of apples

How many barrels and sacks are in the store room?

barrels .... sacks ....

Which goose has laid an egg?

Sheep are kept near the castle.
Which two sheep below aren't eating grass?

Draw more curls on the sheep.

Sheep .... and .... aren't eating.

People in the castle eat fish as well as meat. The fish are kept in a pond. Draw more fish in the pond below.

Amazing armour

Write the names of the parts of this knight's armour, using the words in the list.

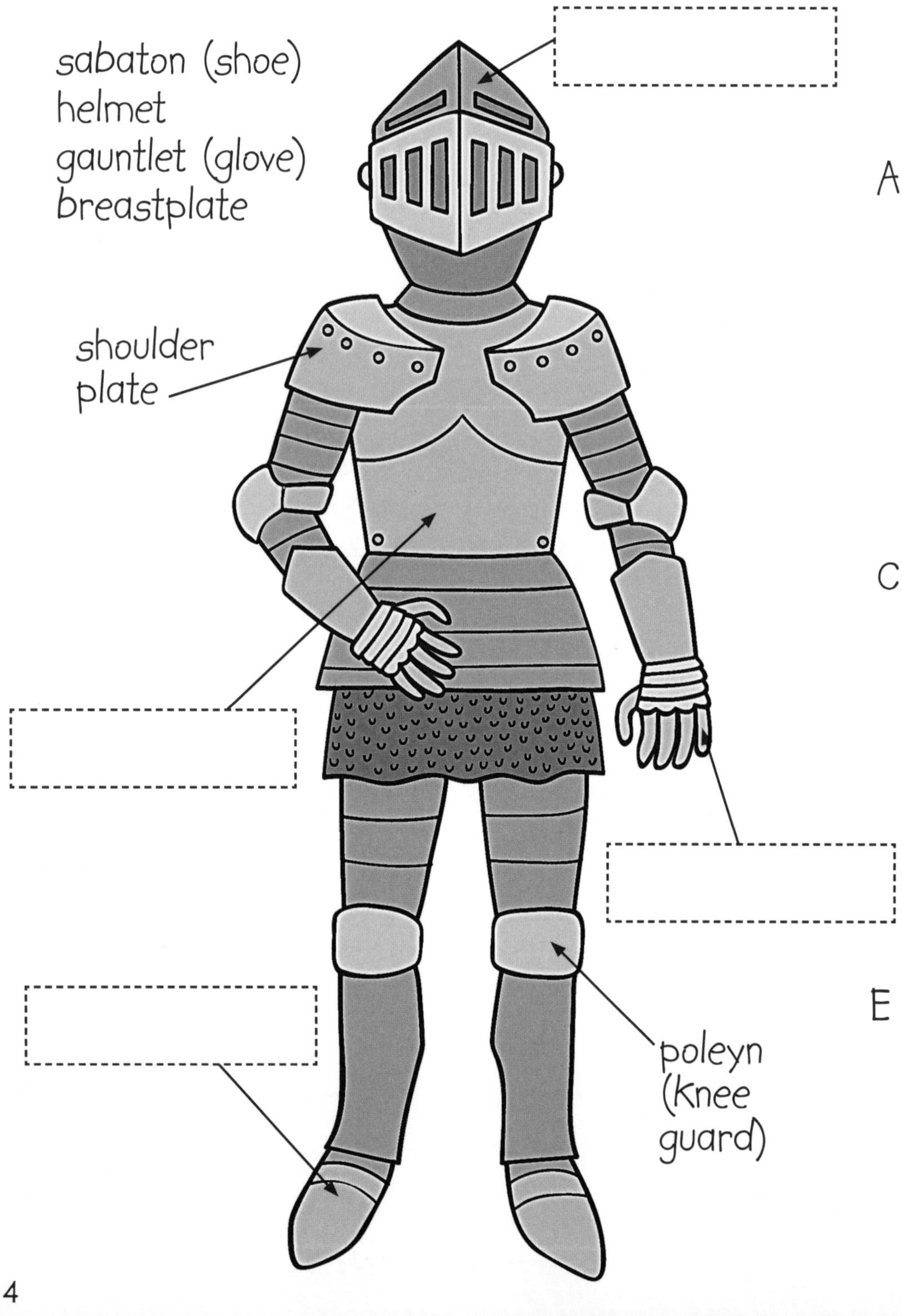

Which two knights have the same armour?

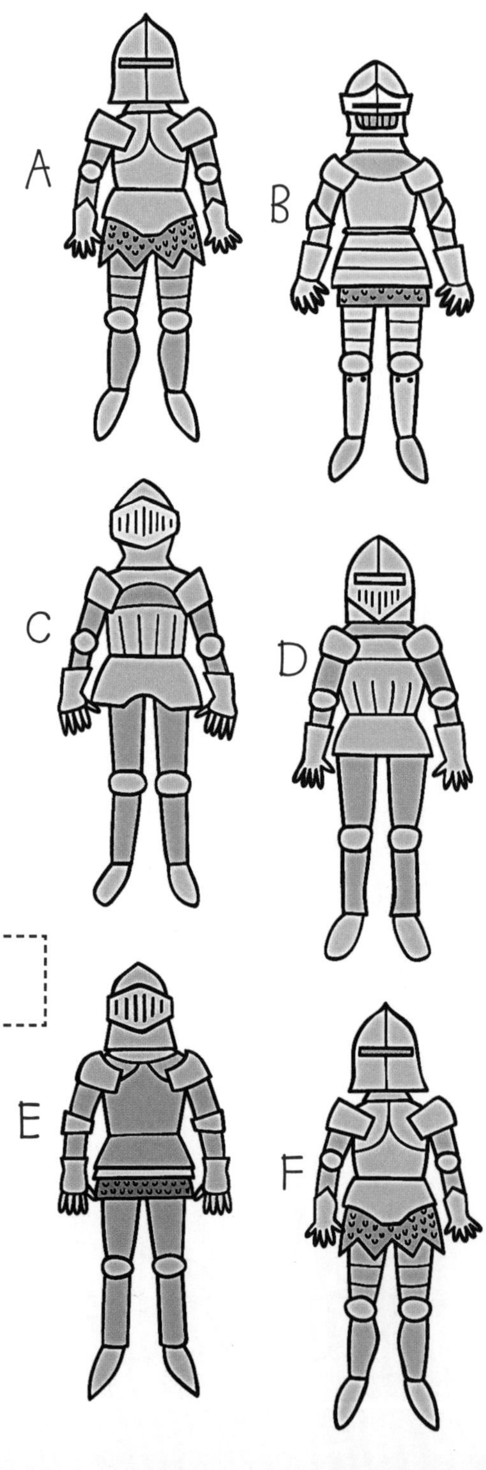

Using the stickers from the sticker pages, give each knight a helmet.

Draw the other half of this knight's armour.

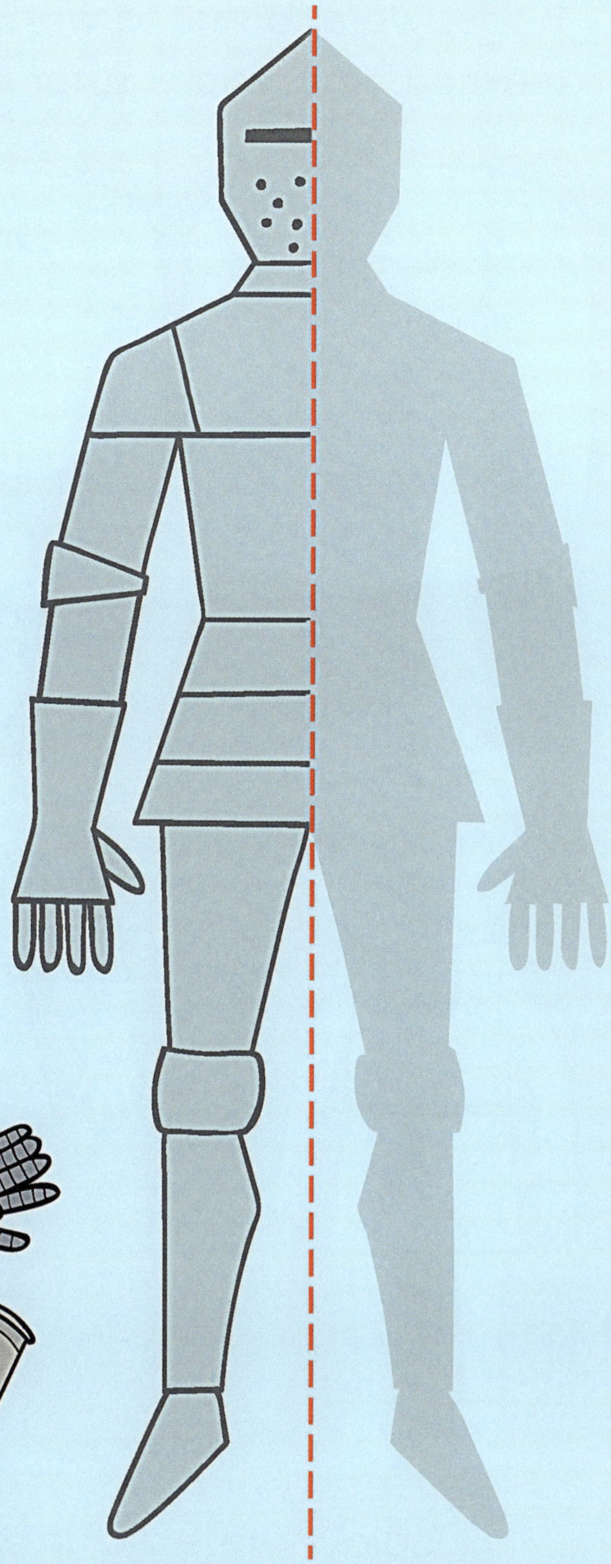

How many matching pairs of gauntlets are there below?

....

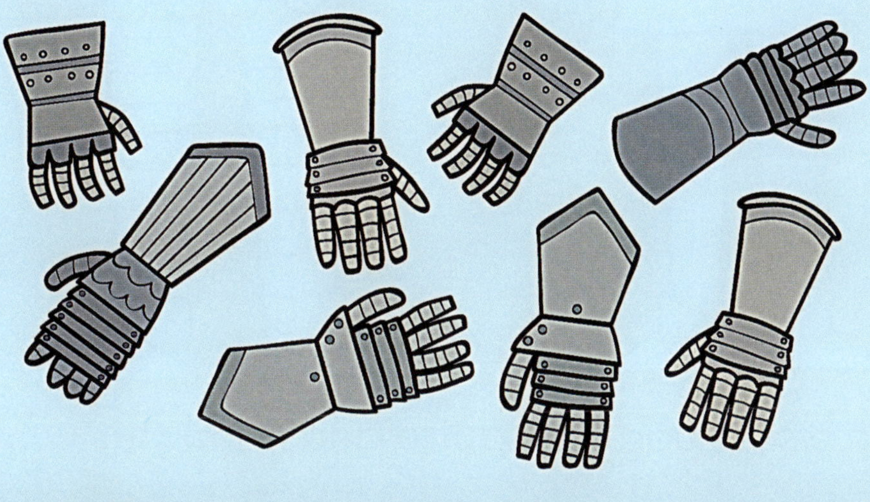

Knight school

Training to be a knight started early. Young boys known as pages were taught to work hard, ride and fight. Later, they learned how to look after a knight.

Colour these pictures of a page, a squire and a knight.

Cedric is a page who is training to be a squire. There's lots to do and learn. Can you spot him?

- He's holding a wooden sword.
- He has fair hair.
- He has a green cap.

One page has fallen asleep. Can you find him?

Which sword does the squire give to the knight?

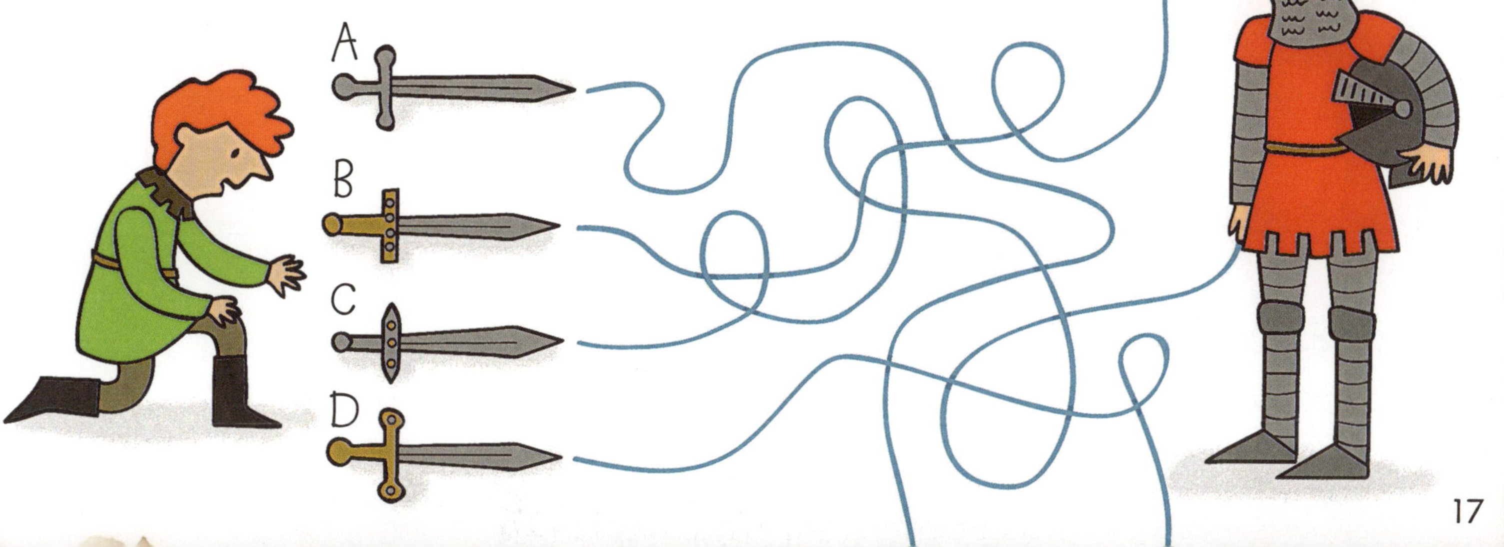

Stinky stuff

It was smelly and filthy in castles. There were lots of animals, and people didn't wash much. Draw a line to link each of the stinky descriptions below to the correct picture.

ROTTEN FOOD
There were no fridges, so the food went bad.

STINKING TOILETS
Everything just dropped down inside the walls into a pit or the castle moat.

PONGY PEOPLE
People didn't wash themselves or their clothes very often.

A

B

C

D

E

SMELLY ANIMALS
There were dirty cats, and dogs... and rats!

FILTHY FLOORS
When the rushes on the floor got too dirty, they were brushed up and replaced.

Bathtime

It's bathtime in the castle. Servants are bringing lots of buckets of hot water to pour into a big wooden tub. Can you spot eight differences between the two pictures?

The hunt

A knight is hunting with his family, friends and servants.

How many people and how many dogs are there altogether?

people .... dogs ....

Count all the spears. ....

Can you find a deer, hiding from the hunt?

Falcons were trained to hunt birds. The one below has just flown away from its handler. Which bird does it catch?

Which two wild boars are exactly the same?

Knights and ladies

Complete these pictures of knights and ladies using the head, body and leg stickers from the sticker pages.

These knights are thinking about their ladies.
Draw lines linking each couple.

Which knight is holding a rose? ....

What to wear

People in castles wore different kinds of clothes.
Draw a line to link each person to the correct word.

knight | lady | page | cook

Colour these people who live or work in a castle.
Use pens that match the spots.

Gregory is already wearing his armour. Godwin's squire is helping him to put his armour on. Is there everything he needs?

Telling tales

Knights liked to tell stories of their adventures and bravery. Some stories were true, but some might have been made up.

The knight below saved a lady from a wicked knight, who had kidnapped her. Which way did he go?

This knight is telling a tale of fighting a dragon. Which one is he talking about? When you've worked it out, colour the dragons.

Busy knight

This knight has lots to do. Many people come to see him to discuss business, ask for help and sort out arguments. Using stickers from the sticker pages, add more people waiting to see him.

Below are pictures of people the knight helped on different days. On which day did he help most people?

He helped most people on ....

The knight is welcoming guests who are visiting the castle. Can you spot six differences between the two pictures?

When the knight's jobs are done, he spends time with his family. Put them in height order, writing 1 next to the shortest person, and 5 next to the tallest.

Up high

Castles on high ground were easier to keep safe. Enemy soldiers want to climb the hill and attack this castle. Can they reach it?

YES / NO

Which square is missing from this picture of a clifftop castle?

A

B

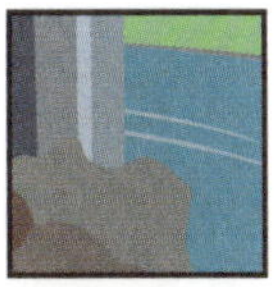

C

D

A sentry is keeping watch on the battlements of a castle. Which view can he see?

A

B

C

Music and minstrels

How many minutes does each of these minstrels sing or play?
Write the answers to the sums below them to find out.

A

5 + 2 = ...

B

6 – 1 = ...

C

3 + 3 = ...

D

7 – 4 = ...

One of these minstrels has lost his instrument.
Can you spot him and can you find the instrument?

A strong fortress

Pages 2-3

Lots of castles

Pages 10-11

Amazing armour

Pages 14-15

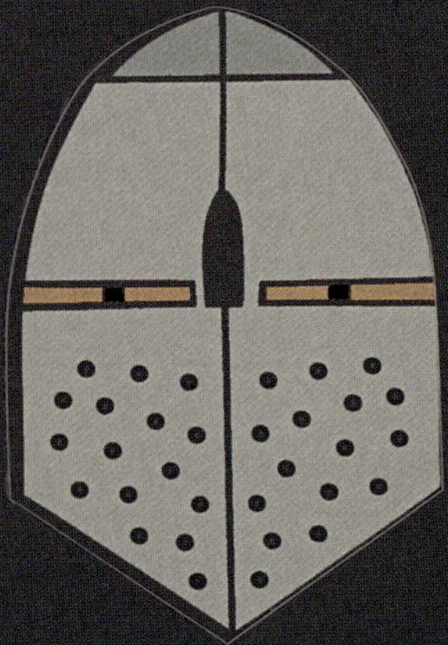

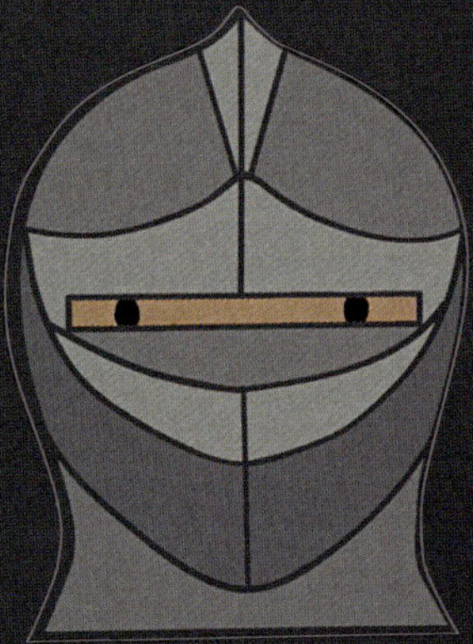

Knights and ladies Pages 22-23

Busy knight Pages 28-29

Big battle Pages 34-35

Castle life Pages 40-41

Castle animals Pages 46-47

Coats of arms Pages 50-51

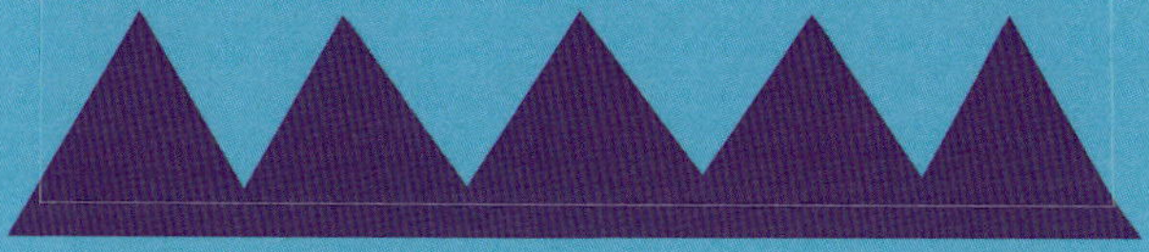

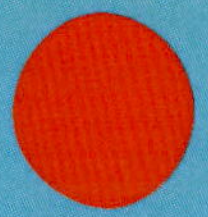

At a tournament Pages 56-57

Jolly jester

Jesters made people laugh by telling jokes. Draw smiling faces on the people, then colour them and the jester.

Big battle

Fill this battlefield with the stickers from the sticker pages.

Soldiers fighting on foot

This knight is on horseback.

A knight has been knocked off his horse. He will have to continue fighting on foot.

This knight is swinging an axe at his enemy.
Arrows flying through the air
An archer firing arrows

In the kitchen

The cook needs all the ingredients in the list to make a stew. Read the list and look at the picture. Is anything missing?

YES / NO

- carrot
- onions
- water
- meat
- cabbage
- peas

Colour these vegetables, using pens or pencils that match the spots.

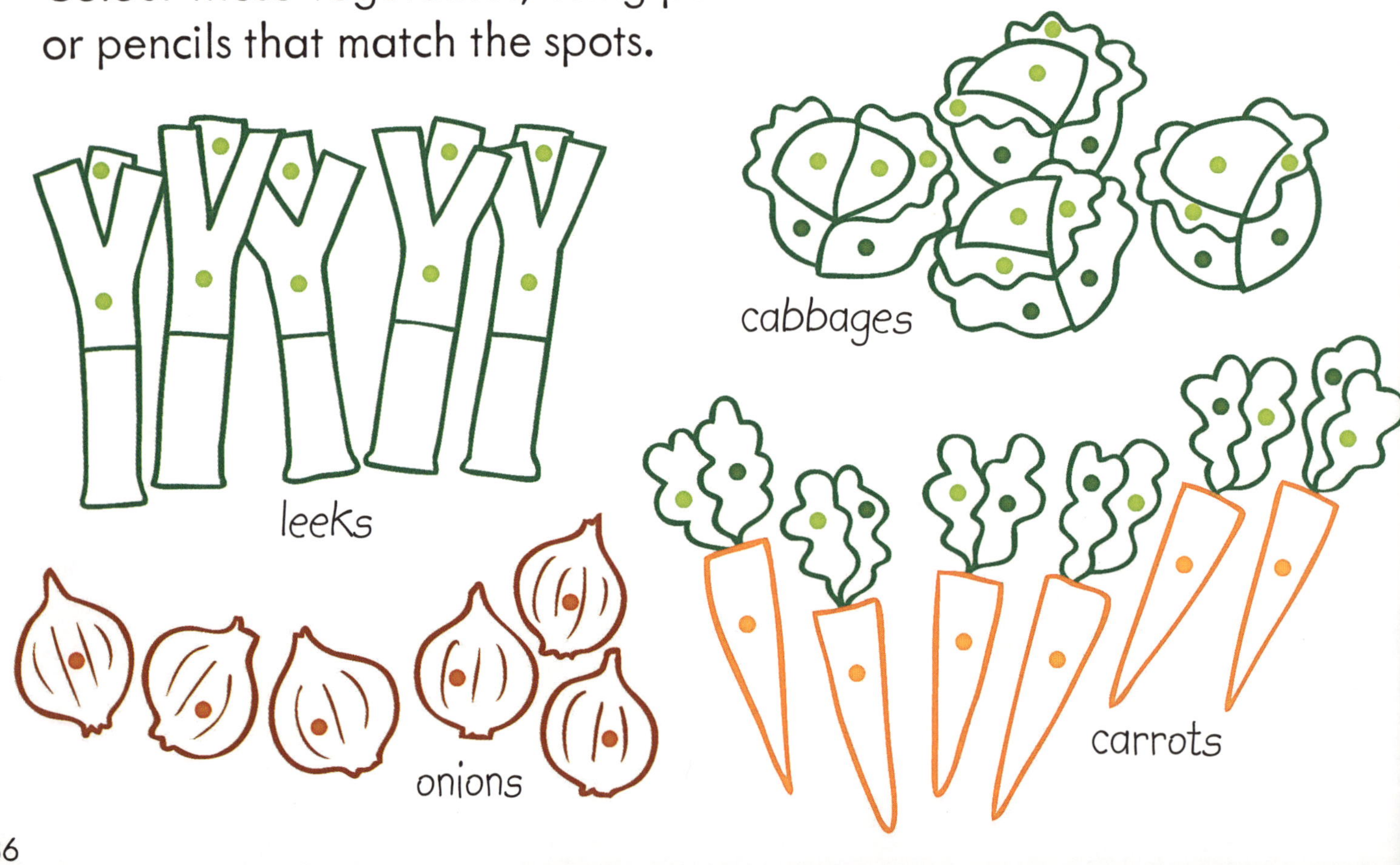

Chickens are roasting on a spit in front of a huge fire. Which two are exactly the same?

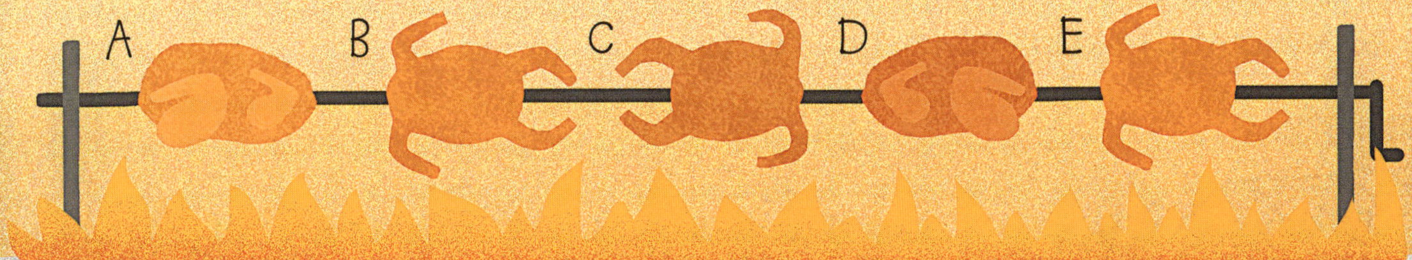

These servants are preparing food on a big wooden table. There are six hungry mice in the picture – can you spot them?

Oops! A bone has fallen on the floor. Which dog eats it?

In the forest

Which way does this hungry stag need to go to eat all the tufts of tasty grass?

Write the names of these creatures using the words in the list.

- wolf
- pigeon
- boar
- deer
- rabbit

How to draw a rabbit:

1. Draw a head and a body.

2. Add ears and a tail.

3. Draw eyes, a nose, a mouth and whiskers.

Draw more rabbits in this space.

There's something different about one of the foxes. Which one?

Castle life

There are lots of rooms in this castle, but four of them are empty. Find the correct stickers on the sticker pages and stick them on. Then, colour the rest of the rooms.

great chamber
kitchen

Draw a castle

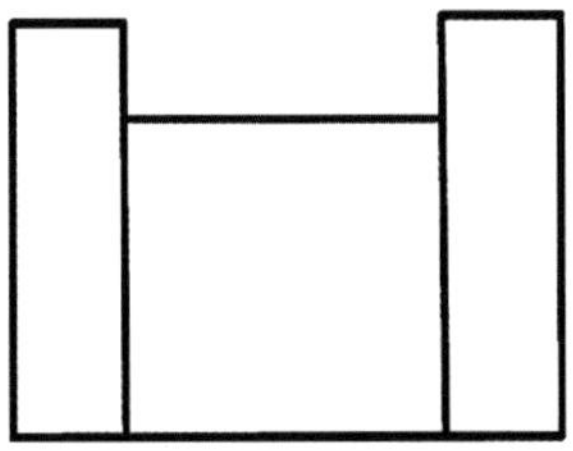

1. Draw a square. Add two towers, one on each side.

2. Draw a tower on top of the castle. Add roofs and flags.

3. Draw an arch for a door. Add some crosses for windows.

Tapestry

Many castles had pictures called tapestries on the walls. Tapestries were woven from lots of coloured threads. Colour this tapestry using pens or pencils that match each spot.

A big banquet

There's a fantastic feast in the Great Hall. Can you spot...

...a juggler?

...4 loaves of bread?

...a servant carrying a jug?

...3 minstrels playing musical instruments?

How many candles are lit?
....
...2 steaming pies?
...a dog with a tasty bone?

Castle animals

As well as people, there were lots of animals in castles. Dogs were used for hunting and lived in kennels. Draw spots on some of these dogs and colour the others.

Falcons were used for hunting, too. They lived in a building called a mews. Can you spot five differences between these two pictures?

Horses lived in stables and were looked after by stable boys. Find the horse stickers on the sticker pages, then add them to the stable.

Join the dots from 1 to 10 to find out what this cat is chasing.

Chickens were kept for eggs and food. How many are there?

....

Under attack

Can you spot ten differences between this castle picture...

...and this one? Draw around each difference you spot.

Coats of arms

Every knight had a different pattern on his shield. This was his coat of arms. Who has copied Edmund's coat of arms?

Colour these shields, using pens or pencils that match each spot.

Decorate this shield, using the stickers from the sticker pages.

The shields below all have different pictures on them. Draw a line to link each shield to the word that describes it.

moons | bear | stripes | dragon | roses

Which knight does the shield below belong to? Read the clues and see if you can work it out.

- *He's not the tallest knight.*
- *He doesn't have brown hair.*
- *He's smiling.*

One section of this shield is blank. Which piece will complete it?

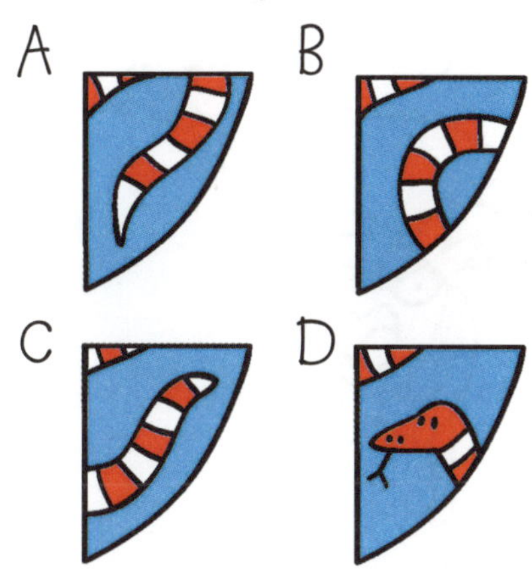

Jumping and juggling

Colour these pictures of acrobats and jugglers who have come to entertain the people of the castle.

Spot a juggler who has dropped a ball.

Find two acrobats in the same position.

Spot someone who's juggling apples.

Colour the rest of these juggling balls, following the sequence of colours.

How many jugglers are there altogether?

....

Colour this acrobat to match his partner.

Castle garden

The lady of the castle wants to go to the herb garden. Which way should she go?

How many pears are on this tree? ....

Which rose bush is different?

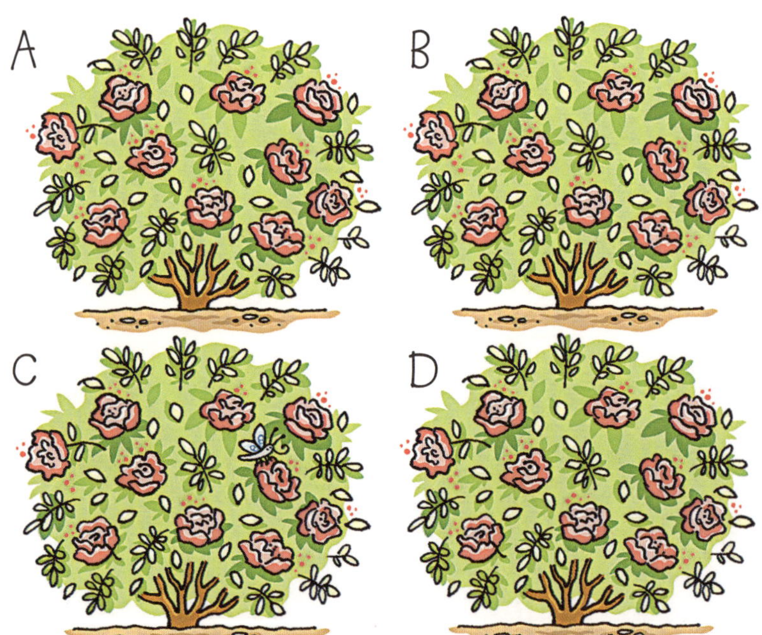

Which order should these pictures of an apple tree be in? Number them from 1 to 4. The first one has been done for you.

Can you spot what's missing from picture B?

At a tournament

Two knights are jousting. Can you spot these people watching?

• a man with a gold chain • a lady in a green dress • someone yawning

Colour the knights and their horses.

red and white

green and orange

yellow and white

Find the tent stickers on the sticker pages. Press each one onto the shape it matches.

Which two of the spectators below are twins?

This man is selling pies. How many does he have?

....

Coming home

Help this knight return to his castle by drawing a line along the path as quickly as you can. Try not to touch the sides.

This knight left for a battle months ago and now he's almost home. Can you spot five differences between the two pictures?

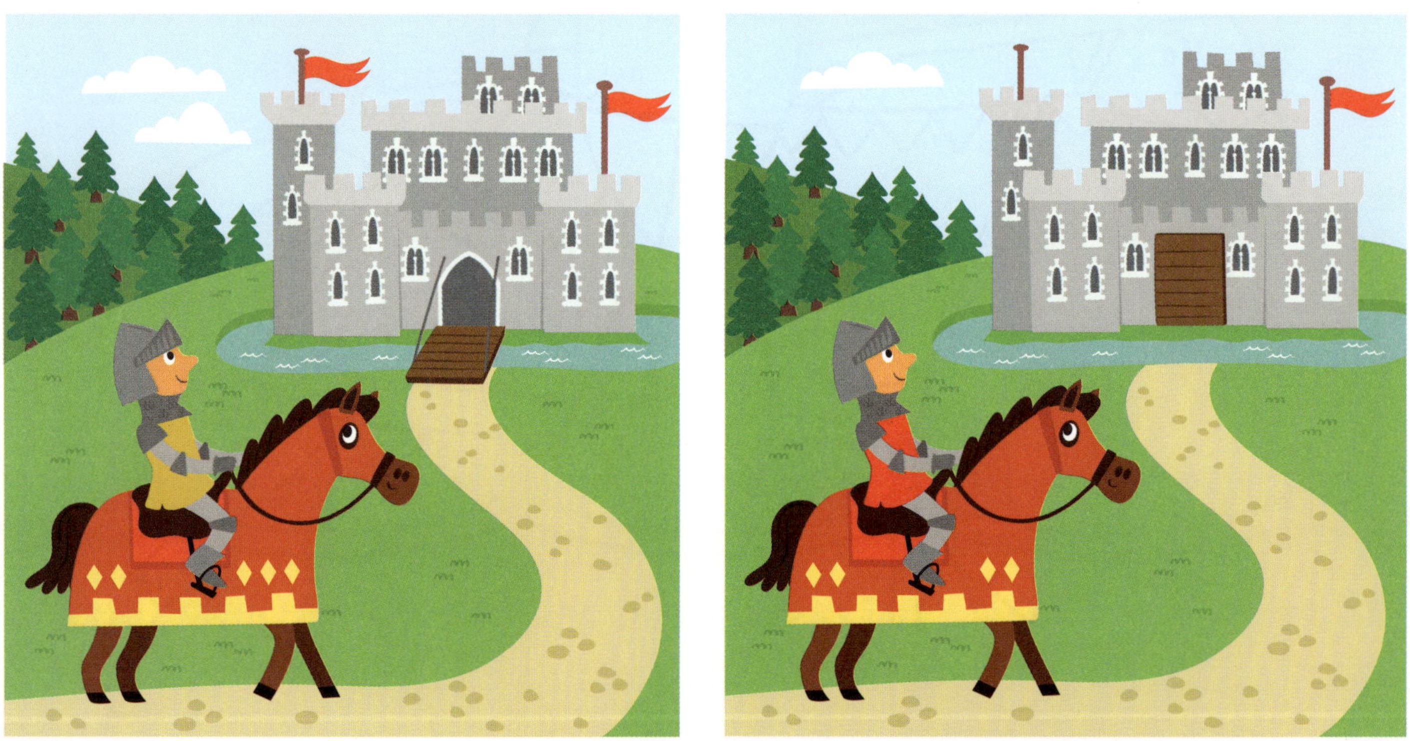

Now that this knight is home, he wants to see his wife. Which way does he need to go, to find her?

Night-time

It's dark in the castle, and someone is standing in front of the fire. Who is it?

The knight and lady need to get to their bed in the great chamber. Which way do they need to go?

Answers

2–3 A strong fortress

Tower D is tallest.

◯ lady looking out of a window

◯ There are 9 soldiers.

6–7 Out and about

Knight C is going to the castle.

8–9 Busy courtyard

◯ man chopping wood —  4 ◯

◯ woman with a basket —  5 ◯

◯ children with a ball —  1 ◯

◯ busy blacksmith —  6 ◯

It would have been noisy in the castle.

10–11 Lots of castles

◯ The knight passes 8 trees.

No, he doesn't cross a stream.

12–13 Castle supplies

No – nothing is missing from the list.
There are 7 barrels and 5 sacks.
Goose B has laid an egg.
Sheep 2 and 7 aren't eating grass.

14–15 Amazing armour

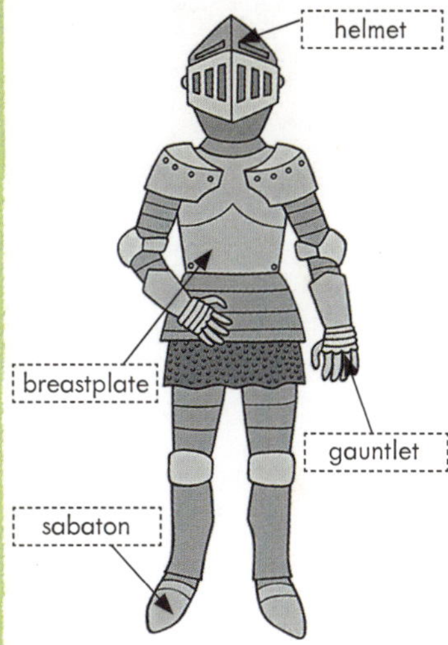

Knights A and F have the same armour.

There are 3 matching pairs of gauntlets.

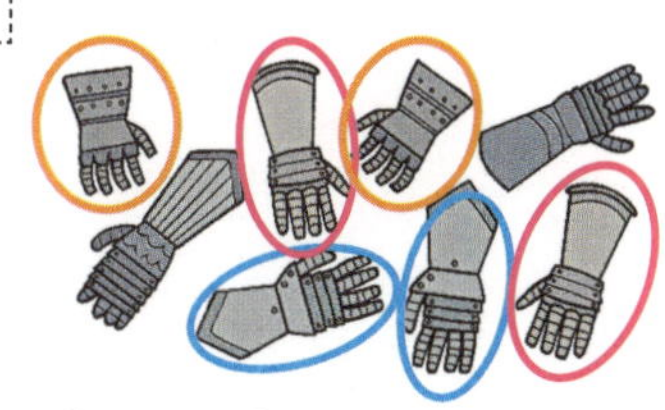

16–17 Knight school

◯ Cedric

◯ sleeping page

The squire gives sword C to the knight.

18–19 Stinky stuff/Bathtime

A = floors
B = animals
C = toilets
D = people
E = food

20–21 The hunt

There are 10 people...

...and 7 dogs.

There are 6 spears.

deer

The falcon catches bird D.

Boars B and F are the same.

22–23 Knights and ladies

Henry is holding a rose.

24–25 What to wear

Yes, Godwin has everything he needs.

26–27 Telling tales

The knight is talking about this dragon.

28–29 Busy knight

He helped most people on Thursday.

You should number the members of the family from left to right: 4, 5, 3, 1, 2

30–31 Up high

No – none of the paths lead to the castle, so the soldiers can't reach it.

Square B is missing from the picture.

The sentry can see view B.

32 Music and minstrels

A plays for 7 minutes, B for 5 minutes, C for 6 minutes, and D for 3 minutes.

This minstrel has lost his instrument.

missing instrument

36–37 In the kitchen

Yes – the water is missing.
Chickens B and E are the same.

◯ mice

Dog C eats the bone.

38–39 In the forest

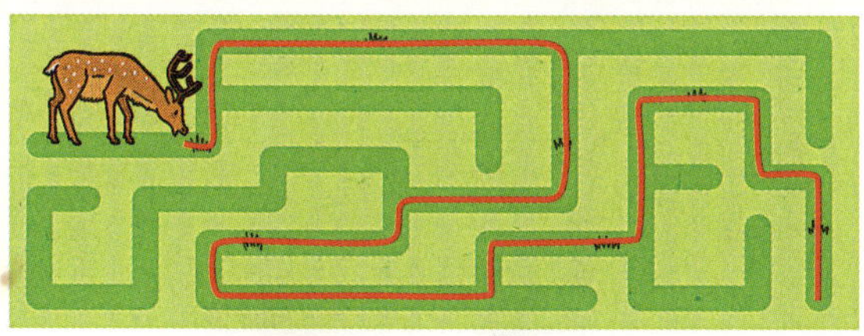

Fox D is different – the tip of its tail isn't white.

44–45 A big banquet

◯ juggler

◯ bread

◯ servant

◯ minstrels

◯ pies

◯ dog

◯ 6 candles are lit.

46–47 Castle animals

The cat is chasing a mouse.

There are 6 chickens.

48–49 Under attack

50-51 Coats of arms

Walter has copied the coat of arms.

The shield belongs to knight B.

Piece C will complete the shield.

52-53 Jumping and juggling

dropped ball

juggling apples

same position

There are 7 jugglers.

54-55 Castle garden

There are 7 pears on the tree.

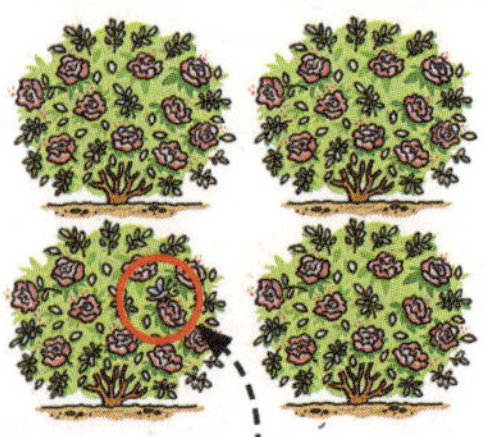

Rose bush C is different – there is a butterfly on it.

A worm is missing from picture B.

56-57 At a tournament

someone yawning

lady in green dress

man with chain

Spectators A and D are twins.

The man has 7 pies.

58-59 Coming home

60 Night-time

C is standing in front of the fire.

First published in 2015 by Usborne Publishing Ltd., Usborne House, 83-85 Saffron Hill, London EC1N 8RT, England. www.usborne.com